Home and Variations

ROBERT ARCHAMBEAU was born in the USA, but grew up in Canada. He studied literature at the University of Manitoba and the University of Notre Dame and has taught at Notre Dame and Lund University (Sweden). He currently teaches at Lake Forest. A chapbook of poetry and a study of postmodern Irish poetry, *Another Ireland*, were published by Wild Honey Press. He has also edited two books, *Word Play Place: Essays on the Poetry of John Matthias* and *Vectors: New Poetics*. He is the editor of the international poetry review *Samizdat*.

Also by Robert Archambeau

Poetry
Citation Suite (Bray: Wild Honey Press, 1997)

Criticism
Another Ireland (Bray: Wild Honey Press, 1997)

As Editor
Word Play Place: Essays on the Poetry of John Matthias
(Athens: Swallow Press, 1998)
Vectors: New Poetics (Lake Forest: Samizdat Editions, 2001)

Home and Variations

Robert Archambeau

Cambridge

PUBLISHED BY SALT PUBLISHING
PO Box 937, Great Wilbraham, Cambridge PDO CB1 5JX United Kingdom
PO Box 202, Applecross, Western Australia 6153

First published 2004

Printed and bound in the United Kingdom by Lightning Source

Typeset in Swift 9.5 / 13

ISBN 1 84471 049 1 paperback

SP

1 3 5 7 9 8 6 4 2

for Valerie, for John, for Michael, and for Ben

Contents

Home and Variations   3
For Possession: Manitoba Barbed Wire, 1885   5
Two Short Films on the translation of the European
    imagination to America   6
Victory Over the Sun   10
Two for Victoria Regina, Her Sages and Satanic Mills   12
Turkish Engraving   14
Annie Oakley Misses the Kaiser   15
The Write Rose: Haiku   16
Blackberry   17
Two for John Matthias   18
Waiting for the Barbarians   20
The Colossus   22
This Ample Earth   23
Masculinity: Improvisations   25
In the Beginning   26
Poem for a War Poet, Poem for a War   27
Misremembering Szymborska   28
The Ships of Jan Vermeer   30
Aubade   32
The People's Republic of Sleepless Nights   33
The Opera, Stopped   34
A Long-Lapsed Catholic in South Bend   36
Like a Skein of Loose Silk Blown Against a Wall   37
Five of the Sun   38
A Birthday Evening   39
Experimental Researches on the Irrational
    Embellishment of Chicago   40

Nightmare, Dream and Bourgeoisie: A Prospect 42
Citation Suite 44
Imitations and Collage: from the Poems of Jules Supervielle 72
Imitations and Collage: from the Poems of Blas De Otero 77
The Frozen Thames 83
Major Thel 91
In Elsinore 97
The Poet, as Professor, Dreams 103

Acknowledgments

Some of these poems have appeared in the following publications: *ACM*; *Crowd*; *InPrint Anthology*; *The Mississippi Review*; *nd[re]view*; *New Voices Anthology*; *The Notre Dame Review*; *The Possibility of Language*; *Potion*; *The Potomac*; *Rattle*; *The Rhubarbarian*; *Tusitala*. "Citation Suite" originally appeared as a limited-edition chapbook from Wild Honey Press. The image accompanying "The Frozen Thames" is reprinted from *The Print in Stuart Britain 1603–1689*, ed. Anthony Griffiths, London: British Museum Press, 1998.

"Home and Variations,"

that is to say:
  the first home and its variations
  as we move from it with it and to it
and:
  variations, as in music—
  a theme or score or text or style, worked and reworked
  until it feels like home.

Home and Variations

Some stay in one place.
Others move. Still others move
from place to place, staying
for a while. But some
stay in one. And if they think of this,
they call it "home." Stop.
And if those who stay in one place
and know it are at home, others, moving, or
moving place to place to stay
and move, are not.
And if they know it, know
they're not at home. Stop.
And if they stayed in one place and moved on
and if they know it, then they know that
when they hadn't moved, they were at home.
Whether they knew it. Whether they not.
Stop.
And if they left and know they left
they feel a lack.
And others stay in one place. And if
they stay and the place won't stay as
the place they knew was the place that's "home" they feel
a lack. Stop. And this tells.
And some who feel a lack will fill
the lack they feel. Stop. And my father
played the phonograph. Played sea chanteys,
played Hank Snow. Played them till my mother,
or went and played them till they stopped. Stop. Played
at being with the sailors, played at being
with Hank Snow. Played at doing what
they did, which wasn't play. Stop. If work
was what men did with hands and tools
on farm and sea and if my father's father worked
with hands and tools but didn't sing. Would the

Here's the idea that invests the poem deepest

singing of the sailors would the singing of Hank Snow
be singing so my father he could play at
being home. Stop. And if his son who moved, and
moved from place to place. Whether he wanted.
Whether he not. If he thought of father thinking father
thinking work and farm and home would
the thinking take him farther would the thinking take him
     home.

Is this the point of his entire approach: to
explore his father's pattern of coming and
going, his own feelings of home given it was
at times with his father and at times
not. And his own tendency to move
from place to place, his own tendency
in his work to travel from ~~plac~~
one idea to another and continually
circle back with pieces of the ideas familiar
combining and disbursing, (until the elements are "being worked
and reworked until it feels like home"
It plays with and explores the notion of home
of how things become familiar, until they feel
like home?

[4]

For Possession: Manitoba Barbed Wire, 1885

take and
use just this single
wire line, for now, urging on to
some ragged stop, tied or
fastened as best you
can, tenuous on the
perpendicular earth, let the wire line
sing, a low howl with
the wind, to mark also
by sound our quiet
divisions, to say that we are
on this ground

This is a meditation (variation?) on the barbed wire and the meaning / insight it provide of those who put it up.

the Cree the Blackfoot the Métis

the Cree the Blackfoot the Métis

[handwritten: I'm not sure he's adding much perspective beyond simply putting these 2 men together]

Two Short Films
on the translation of the European imagination to America

> ... what we feel of sorrow and despair
> From ruin and from change, and all the grief
> The passing shews of being leave behind,
> Appeared an idle dream ....
>
> WORDSWORTH, The Prelude

> Up to now literature has exalted a pensive immobility, ecstasy, and sleep. We intend to exalt aggressive action, a feverish insomnia ...
>
> MARINNETI, Futurist Manifesto

[handwritten: Not much here / except / poetic / description]

1. WORDSWORTH AT THE CUYAHOGA'S MOUTH, 1796–1996

In newsreel stock, in jumpy monochrome
You mount the windy bluff, glance back and turn
To face the valley. Far below, white water foams

Birds cry, and black waves peel from slabs of rock,
Back down to the great lake's boom and suck.
You stand, a silhouette, black coat and stick.

The film moves quickly now—clouds fly and light's
A flickered blur of days and nights. You wait,
The still point of a world that's turned to haste.

You wait, and plowed lines break the dark earth's crust—
The valley peopled now—and frontier huts
Crop up each harvest time. A rail line thrusts

On past that limestone ridge, with quick faint wraiths
That, caught in a frame that stutters through the gate,
Are horses, wagons, wide-backed men. You wait,

Brick chimneys frame the screen and black smoke swells,
A furnace-city churns its molten steel—
And one quick night's a flash: city plays hell.

And you, above this growth and flux and ruin,
Does your sleepwalker-muse fetch Whitman songs
Great port, great ore-port, great handler of iron —

Or bring *an image of tranquility*
So calm and still, a green dream's tapestry
Of soft grass overgrowing history?

I can't expect an answer: You stand, there,
And breathe the flickered light of setting suns, the living air.

2. MARINNETI AT UNION STATION, CHICAGO

Arrived, the locomotive paws the track,
deep-chested, bellowing

(we gather, from this silent reel);
its steam-plumes jet in cavern air

beneath the city. And, arrived—
in the city of railyards,

apparatus, of stokers groping blackened
through the mill-fire's angry blast,

the city of shipping, chemical manufacture,
stockyards blazed with electric moons—you,

mounting the platform, gestures broad,
erratic, oratorical.

Saying (we barely see, white letters
over faded stock) *Hold no ideal mistress high,*

her form divine rising to touch clouds;
saying *All must be swept aside,*

to express our whirling life of steel, of pride,
of fever and exalted speed;

saying, in that rush of sailors, workmen,
quick-eyed thieves, *death to Ciceroni, antiquarians* . . .

Mechanic-limbed and darting, the crowd
won't pause to hear you, and I

wonder, do you dream of Venice,
soft, past-loving, shocked

in all her statuary, when you declared
The first dawn is now, an explosive breath?

You, erratic, oratorical, the last frame
fading on your words, *our bodies die for speed*

for movement and for darting light.

Victory Over the Sun

Here come the Futurists.
One wears a spoon in his buttonhole.

One signs an unknown hieroglyph.
One sings vowels, another consonants.

Here come the Futurists. It is 1913.
Kruchenykh, Matiushin, Goncharova,

Burliuk who leads his giant brother,
"I-Burliuk" on both their brows.

Here come the Futurists. Come, Kazemir Malevich,
saying "let the familiar recede,

let all by which we've lived
be lost to sight."

They come. Let all by which they've lived
be lost to sight—

let Moscow, drunk, serf-shouldered,
(a stunted mongrel, a cold and coal-blacked thief)

be lost. The massing of troops,
the Czar who calls a madman to heal his bleeding son,

the hunger,
the boy who beats his brother in a tailor's grimy shop—

let these recede, be lost to sight. —repetition
Here come the Futurists. It is 1913.

With a flash, a clash of metal, projectors flash again: *is this necessary*
They have begun.

They sing of victory over all we know,
a roar against the daily sun. ✔

Then it is 1914, 1940, it is Moscow, Leningrad,
the Gulag, Buchenwald, it is the exile's empty room,

a daughter, grieving.
Here come the Futurists, long gone into the dark

with their victory over the sun.

H

Two for Victoria Regina, Her Sages and Satanic Mills

1. PATER AND HIS AGE

In coke fire, in kiln: accumulation.
In furnace, in engine, in black iron machine,
In loom-thrum, train clatter, in sulfur and mine shaft,
In ash from brick chimneys comes surplus, comes hoard.

Percussion cap, cartridge, hard black hands of miners,
Blasting of rock face, quick flash, hissing fuse;
Engineer, steel wheel, white sparks from hard braking,
Embankment, blue gas light, slum child, rank canal.

Consumption in cough and in candelabra,
Excess in the watch-chain's long droop to the fob,
Use-value in square fingered hands warmed at ashcans
Whose fires light tight tangled streets without names.

And would I, too, flee the moralist's preaching
To burn with the light of a hard, gem-like flame?

2. HERNE HILL

[handwritten: again telegraphing his values]

A hill made tame by monied speculation
Was his full world, his father's careful Eden
In iris, in lilac, in richest viburnum.

In the mulberry south, past the wrought-iron gate,
Away from the century's engine, from soot,
From the piston-stroke, the flywheel's scattered light,

He grew, creation of his mother's hopes:
At nine, he noted types and anti-types;
Glibly said each yeoman was an Adam, free to take

[handwritten: look here up]

From creation, and when his mother sang
She was Hannah, just as the Sunday throng
Were the lost tribes, united in brisk forthright songs—

But who were the hard men who, battered yet balanced,
Trained engines' sinews to strict new cadences?
No answer. Precocious Ruskin found his silences.

Turkish Engraving

~ / √

Were they wrong about decline, those men
Who etched in copper urbane scenes? These plates
Of coffeehouses, streets, the marketplace,
Interstices of life, should these condemn
Their makers, who saw days fill up with talk
And trade, backgammon, dark flirtatious eyes,
Hands nimbly plucking strings to song—all while
They knew the armies fled the field, exports dropped,
And rats' feet crept on dozing tramps down by the quays?
Perhaps they felt the measure of decay
Too large to matter much. Each, in his way
Could capture pleasures, living privately.
Good coffee steams in our cafés and we, like them,
Hide hunger for solutions from our friends.

Annie Oakley Misses the Kaiser

and what if she didn't?
In a clover field somewhere in September in a war
a corporal finds three cigars and a master plan for all the south—
Lee's dream of victory—left by a dreaming young officer dreaming of
peace and what if he didn't? Wilkes Booth in the wings steels his nerve,
waits for the cue, and the curtain drops before the play begins, *Exeunt.*
Annie Oakley misses the Kaiser.

Annie Oakley misses the Kaiser, who pulled,
from the gold case, his cigar, waved off the police. In a clover field
   somewhere
Wilkes Booth dreams at peace, the great Khan's son is dead—
brilliant, drunk, humane and dead, back in twelve-hundred forty two,
and armies flee unravaged Vienna to attend his funeral and
what if they didn't? At the Wild West Show, wild applause.

Annie Oakley sweats in her buckskins when the Kaiser rises
from the grandstand before the planted volunteer. Wilkes Booth sails
for sweet Vienna, strides on the quarterdeck, lights his cigar, *Lusitania*
painted on the prow, the torpedo-trail foams white and far to stern
and what if and what if and what if it didn't?

The train pulls in at Finland Station, risen
from the troubled dream of final peace the bearded man
in London dreams, his child's hungry crying curbs his sleep,
he dozes at his desk, cigar ash down his jacket-front, dreams
the dialectic, inevitable peace, nowhere to go but freedom,
nothing to lose but nothing to lose but what if he didn't dream what if
   he didn't?

Annie Oakley misses the Kaiser, blasts the cigar from his clenched teeth.
Her sweet relief to wild applause. Writes, in 1914,
"may I take a second shot?"

The Write Rose: Haiku

There, in the past tense,
in foliage, verbiage—
the red rose rises.

Rising, the rose rose,
and by any other name
would rise otherwise.

The read rose rises,
its foliage verbiage
by another name.

At the edge of space
fire-fangled syllables
dangle, dangle down.

My love is like a.
Red red rose, my love is like.
This formal, tight, and
                         quick delight.

Blackberry

for Robert Hass

Blackberry, he writes, hoping to have said
all the full, ripe word can say to all who knew
that acrid sweetness on the tongue, once, in summer,
and all who long for those remembered summers.

Blackberry, he writes again, wanting the word,
wanting it to mean all he means when he dreams
of a summer by the live and shimmering rough-shored lake,
the pines rising frail as smoke over the hills
to the robin's-eggshell of the sky; all she meant
with the acrid sweetness of her tongue, that woman
whose arms trembled after making love.

why the hyphen?

Blackberry, he writes, the black ink wet there,
on the page, the full, ripe cursive loops wide,
as if with the weight of hanging fruit.

Blackberry, the full ripe sweetness of it, on his tongue.

Two for John Matthias

[handwritten: This is a rift on a piece(s) by John Matthias but it doesn't add much more than a letter to John]

1. PART SONG

John dot M dot one at nd dot and edu, *[handwritten: his email address]*
(homage, play and letter, plea and midwest place)

[handwritten: line breaks?]

At the big lake's other end and reading "Swell." Glad to see it,
glad you're greedy yet, and leave me greedy, wanting more.
More than three and more than four, we'll publish them,
and hope for more. Glad to see that mini-skirt you saw,
and F. Scott's cock and naked swimmers (noon or midnight)
swimming – where? – near Horton's Bay? It was words
and eros, death was lurking, it was bulls and bullets to the skull.
The cool lake breeze blows from up north and finds me, greedy
    reader, here.
Where Tom Buchanan's ponies played at polo, with the swells.
Where leaves breathe with peace and plenty,
where broad lawns gather narrow minds. The Midwest's own
    East Egg,
in summer, en provence, for sure.
Ice jingles in a tumbler, words tumble from my printer's buzz.
Your poem in three parts, now four. (I'll print them, and I'll
    hope
for more). And his last story of Nick Adams, left unfinished, ends
with promise, ends with "sure." That he'd tell the story, that
    he'd
read and read some more. The lake is swell, the breeze feels
    great,
I like the old man's late, erotic work. Chablis. A bird from
    London. *[handwritten: girl?]*
Lake swells, the breeze from shore.
And my greedy hope is this: I'll say
"Send more." And you'll say "sure."

[18]

No strong attention to form (handwritten)

2. BLACK DOG'S BEDSIDE MANNER

for John Matthias in a losing season,
the black dog depression at his side . . .

The black dog's in the room with you,
and what to do but wait until he bites?
He'll wolf your dinner, spill your whiskey,
piss in the fireplace when you try to write.
He'll bar the door, he'll stretch and lean, stare cross-eyed
at your daughters and then leer at your wife.
He's slipped the Bishop's muzzle, he's gnawed the lawyer's cat.
Despite the best prescriptions, he's made the doctors cough.
The black dog's in your bed with you,   *— key Robert word* (handwritten)
and what to do but wait until he bites?
Spurt-sprinting in his sleep, he dreams you're prey,
caught, clutched and carried, cradled in his gentle jaw back
    home.
In your dream you run from him, or write
"sit, boy" or "beg" or "heel" or "fetch."
And in your dream the black dog takes his bitch.
Beside your bed and fevered sleep
he rests his paw upon your sweating head,
he leans in to hear you muttering
"Play dead, play dead, play dead . . . "

[19]

Waiting for the Barbarians
C. P. Cavafy (slight return)

Waiting, waiting, packed thick in the forum,
we know this: the barbarians are due here today.

We've gathered, our hands grown soft, and thick with rings.
We've gathered, impatient, while the plum tree shadows grow.

Senators, orators, patrician young men
have left their long councils and wait here today,

done with their scheming, their spies,
their tense-browed intrigues,

> *No intrigue will profit*
> *when the barbarians rule.*

The wealthy, relieved, have sent home their guardsmen
and wander careless among the crowd.

> *There will be no thieves, and beggars won't hover*
> *fly-thick around our doorsteps, not when the barbarians come.*

See the priestess on the temple steps,
how she pulls the jewel from her braids and shakes her hair,

how she strides lightly down,
to be among us.

> *The barbarians come, and have no use for mysteries,*
> *so tedious and recondite.*

why this lyric?

The Emperor has had his chair set beneath the plum trees,
and waves off his advisors with their bundles of scrolls.

[20]

What advice can they give? The barbarians come,
and will rule in their fashion, without learned council.

The plebes and the beggars have come, and hover at the edge of
    the forum,
too far for one to read their eyes' expression.

What can they be thinking? Surely they know
their lot will be much improved when the barbarians come.

The plum tree shadows have grown long, and are lost
in the rising darkness. We wait, we wait. I hear a crow

in the frost-hard dawn and see, in that estranging light,
the time has come. Our hair grows long, our robes are shaggy
    cloaks,

our rough hands curl round daggers' hilts.
Cautiously, we eye each other. The barbarians have come at last.

5th Accomplished formally
but could have a bit
more life in the language ✓

The Colossus

variation on a theme from Plath

Slant
rhymes ←

The nights grow strange: red stars, plum sky.
I never shall repair him properly.

I shelter in his shattered throat.
At dawn I rise and scoop its gathered silt.

The creased plates of a broken skull
Grow thick with moss, and shelter nests of owls.

I pause among the cypress trees,
Or heft against my chest his bronze-cast eyes.

Wind plays among his fluted bones,
And on that pillared tongue I used to own.

Glue-pot, glue-brush, fine hammer, nails—
I build a scaffold, try to gauge the size,

The heft of fragments of that face
That once was mine. I find the lip, embossed

With sneers I knew, from long ago,
Or David carved by Michelangelo.

The nights grow strange: red stars, plum sky.
I never shall repair him properly.

This Ample Earth

This ample earth arcs all between us,
four thousand miles of ocean curve.

In the damp closed-in Scandinavian night,
how not to think of you in our midwestern city,

in a morning with the rush of wind in leaves,
with streaming light ...

I read, I read, I read and drowse
above the passage—Adam thunder-struck,

astonished, there in ample Eden, with his dream, his Eve
there, freshly made—"Thy likeness, thy fit help, thy other self,"

he's told, "thy wish, exactly to thy heart's desire."
The first great sin of all my sex:

a man's dream-story, told
as if a God's. But still

I drowse in all that story's gardens,
amorous prospects, rills and plains,

its rush of wind in leaves,
its streaming light, and know

your gracious purpose in our morning-love,
murmurs, supple well-knit limbs ...

We could talk out all our story, choices, trade-offs, our careers
and how I ended up, or chose to end up, here.

But for now, let the story over which I drowse
be ours, and let me, from these pages, learn

how I will know you, and how adore,
how wake and find you, find you real.

Masculinity: Improvisations

(handwritten: Clever but feels like it is guided by the puns and not, by intention — somewhat — completely)

Women ... must invent the impregnable language that will wreck
partitions, regulations and codes ... .Such is the strength of women that,
sweeping away syntax, breaking that famous thread which acts for men like
a surrogate umbilical cord ...

ELAINE MARKS and ISABELLE DE COURTIVRON

1.

These men
The semen
The S and M
The *esse*, then

(handwritten: very clever)

2.

Ecriture feminine
A creature, *femme*
A creeping seme
The weeping, same

3.

gendered male
Gendarmes all
Les gens de maille
The General ails

In the Beginning

[handwritten: interesting piling of associations to create an impression]

the word was *father* and
the word was *divorce* and the word was *emptied*
and the word was *confessed* and the word
was like water, wide and without sound and
the word was *father* and the word
was *asunder* and the word was
war and the word was *Vietnam* the word
was *fool's-cap-of-feathers* and the
word was *Jerusalem* and the word was *buy low* and
the word was *men-with-bird's-faces* and the word was *sold lower*
and the word was *prescription* and the words *forever, forlorn,*
    forsworn, foreclose
were lurking in the parking lot and the word
was *turtle's back*
and the word was *water*
without form and the word was *buckshot* and *barbed wire* and
    firmament
and the word was *one-shall-be-two* and the word was *divorce*

[handwritten left margin: like playing word puns, alliteration]

[handwritten bottom: Strong use of repetition in form (list poem) with what seem to be unrelated words that pile up to create a powerful personal impression]

Poem for a War Poet, Poem for a War

1.

The lines inked on the map are railways and roads.
The lines on the roads are refugees, and moving.
The lines inked on the page are a poem, your poem.
    While you are singing, who will carry your burden?

The lines on the page are a poem, words
that move toward the refugees, their tattered world
of hurt and proper names, their lost, their staggering.
    While you are singing, while you are singing.

The lines are helpless in this time of war. They survive,
if they are a poem, in valleys of their saying, they survive
and reach for valleys where bodies cough, bleed or stumble
    blind.

They survive while you are singing,
    While you are singing.

2.

The lines on the roads are refugees,
Their paths are marked with ink, charted
on a General's table. Your lines are a poem.
    While you are singing, who will carry your burden?

A woman bends beneath her load, a young man stutters in his
    fear,
A guard at the valley's border lets them through,
or not. Your lines are a poem.
    Who will carry your burden?

I think, Does it warrant attaching itself to
Symborska's poem? Maybe,

Misremembering Szymborska

I read your poem in a magazine, the one about how
after every war, someone

has to tidy up, about how,
as years trudge on with shovel and with trowel,

bridges are rebuilt, windows glazed, doors set back
into their jambs, until someone,

propped broom in an arm's neat crook, a hand-back wiping
at his brow, tells how it was to a nodding neighbor, until

the task-bound crowd of a rebuilt city finds such talk
a little boring,

until those who were there
are gone, and those who knew them, until, at last,

someone lies in the grass, over all the old and rusted arguments,
"a corn stalk in his teeth,

gawking at clouds." I read it, there, but
remembered it differently. Somehow

in the tired and task-bound wearied mind those final,
placid, resting limbs

became a body *in* the earth, not on it,
a corn stalk growing from that place in which it lay.

I see your poem now, again, "The End and the Beginning,"
and know I've carried my mistake for months.

That soldier I remembered—that's what he must have been,
that body under the earth—he would have dreamed

of days spent gawking, on a hillside, at the clouds.
Perhaps he fought for just such days, that he should have them,
      perhaps

that dream is where he lingers even now.
Perhaps he can lie beneath your dreamer, a rightness, there,

each in his way the other's end. Perhaps, too,
we could say my poem lies in the grass of your poem's
      dreaming,

forgetful, pulls at corn stalks, gawks at sky.

[handwritten: very tight, well done]

[handwritten: great poetic title]

[handwritten: good, but small ambition]

The Ships of Jan Vermeer

Have I not yet known you, those times I've watched
Your light breathe peace across a silent chamber,
Your Delft compose itself at water's edge?

I thought you intimate of light's surcease,
The connoisseur of life's mute poise still-life,
Your world no larger than the little streets,

Or that space a girl's quick eyes embrace,
Abandon, pass again. And yet you heard
The rumble as a world rolled loose, displaced

From kings and cosmos by a lens that spied
Too far in fickle Heaven. And you knew
What nature offered, prone upon a slide,

To other lenses, brooding to detect
An image like the land outside of Delft
(Mud-churned, much battled, lunar, derelict).

Did you hear that rumble in your work—
Those soldiers, anxious letters, charts of heaven,
[handwritten: manoeuvred] Charts of seas emblazoned with those bristled arks,

That brisk, *[brisk circled]* set sail out from that Holland coast
(Emigrés, *Boer-brodders*, Huguenots)
The *Roord Zee* century of fleeing masts?

Better to know the little streets, the light
On every brick in Delft. Better, you knew,
To seek the grey in water, blue in slate.

Better to know one window and one chair,
One woman's glance that brushes with your eyes, — *who is this?*
One silent room, the gold light shining there.

Aubade

[handwritten: Look up. Song of lovers separating at dawn]

[handwritten: nice] *[handwritten: ✓]* *[handwritten: a bit presumptous]*

Each morning paws us, all us sleeping dolls,
and wonders if it wants to play

or rend us quick.
If this was always so, I didn't know it,

knowing safety as we still can know *[handwritten: How do we know that?]*
the final breath before each waking—

intimately, unknowingly.
"Oh take me back, take me back"—

a dull needle scratching at one groove, my voice
an ancient gramophone, stuck sputtering, a squawk and squeal.

Still, sometimes we wake up happy, and the universe,
subdued, seems willing to protect us.

And, sometimes, insomniac,
until the night sky ages to a purple bruise,

sometimes, insomniac,
we've all watched some other window's light,

an exile's flare, an ally's beacon,
until it's lost in all the bright and scalding day.

The People's Republic of Sleepless Nights

As if in a cold war spy flick, it is a foggy night.
You pull up to the striped and lowered roadblock
and the checkpoint guard, fat in his overcoat,
breathes gin down your neck as he thumbs through your passport.

He stamps it with the black and oily barn-owl crest.

You know what's through that mountain pass, you've been before.
Insomnia speaks a harsh and stuttered language—
in it all your answers sound like questions—
and on her cobbled capital streets all friends are strangers.

You know what you'll find among the natives:

their milk is black, storms rage in their living-rooms,
bones grow in the tongues of the old, who cannot speak.
The sun burns out his days in exile, pacing a poor and sweaty chamber,
and you, the black-gloved master spy, you light another cigarette.

The guard has waved you through. Your headlights glare like lidless eyes.

The Opera, Stopped

On January 5, 1996, at the Metropolitan Opera House opening of Janacek's "Makropulos Affair," the tenor Richard Versalle fell ten feet from his position on a ladder in the opening scene, and died. The orchestra continued to play for a moment, as if nothing had happened.

1.

A stir, in all that darkened air,
Last coughs, stowed programs, final whisperings
Begin "The Makropulos Affair."
Some came with no more expectation
Than the "feast for burghers," that quick elation
Stolen from the day's long worrying.

Some knew, before, what all would see—
A woman, lived three centuries, gone cold,
Though ever-young, who learns (*sotto voce*)
This "stroke of luck that says that all must end
Gives birth to passion": only death can lend
Us life. These knew they'd leave restored:

What more could one have asked? That death
Should serve this life, that one who could have lived
Should choose to die, like us. Perhaps art's worth
The cost, giving, if not the truth, enough.
Alone amid the crowd that whispers, coughs,
Each patient here waits on this cure for dread.

2.

Janacek, mad with love (at last)
Stirred, from your darkened years, to life,
How could you know no strings, no vocalist,

Not even Capek's play, set into song
Could veil that dread, or weave an argument
That one slip wouldn't tear, and render wrong.

d like the repetitions

3.

One slip, that fall, the obscene lying-there,
The music, veiling nothing, trails to nothing:
Silence. Then a stir, in darkened air.

Nice, It could've been more ✓

A Long-Lapsed Catholic in South Bend
for John D. Caputo

The snow is only the snow
clumping high on spare branches outside that window,

a thick, wet, physical stuff. Yet   *necessary*
you tell and tell your mad, rambling, philosopher's tale,

that once, there was a sun; that once
that sun could hold us all in all its warm and liquid light,

then came the snow—
thick and wet, the roughened pelt

of a rough beast winter, slouching
to its dying-place; then came the snow,   *rep*

                    cremation?
thick and white funereal ashes. You tell of men
beneath the clotting snow that chokes the dark and emptied
    sky,

the small-framed men who seek dry branches
for a small fire's light, for a small fire's heat, where some can
    gather.

And telling, on this snowy night,
you burn, a flame from other suns.

And the snow is only the snow.
And the tale is only a small fire's heat, where some can gather.

[36]

Small but great title

−1✓

Like a Skein of Loose Silk Blown Against a Wall

Parisienne most *formidable*—
      in artifice of *coiffe* and scarf,
      cold mistress of your shoes and poise,
with bags that bear the *Hermès* label—

Your hands are full, and you're unable
      to scratch that itch that plagues your back.
      You, knowing that no one is watching,
Rub up against that nearby maple.

Equine? Bovine? In that black dress?
I smile, and somehow hate you less.

[37]

Five of the Sun

1.

The owl's midnight eye, in day.

2.

My enemy, risen early,
to find me where I sleep.

3.

Brute roar and shaggy mane,
brute roar and claw-clutched crimson orb,
heraldic, ancient, gold-wrought lion.

4.

Whispers in red wheat
at dawn.
Whispers in red wheat
at dusk.

5.

Admiring father of my hearth-fire,
my candle's flame his pampered daughter,
indulgent master of the fattened moon,
and, among the gathered stars,
a poor and distant cousin.

[38]

A Birthday Evening

and,
in the window-glass, the first
outline-apparition:
my ghost, across the green world's growth.

OK but would like to have been wilder

Experimental Researches on the Irrational Embellishment of Chicago
i.m. André Breton, his city and his schemes

Should one preserve, modify, change or suppress:

The Water Tower

> *Place it underwater off the easternmost point of Navy Pier. Replace it with a seventy-foot high barber pole.*

Buckingham Fountain

> *Fill the fountain daily with gold coins bearing Mayor Daley's saying from the 1968 Democratic National Convention, "To Preserve the Existing Disorder." They are free for the taking.*

The Picasso

> *Destroy it and use the scrap metal to build many tiny wind-up toys in the shape of Al Capone. Release these on Daley Plaza under a banner reading "A Local Pride."*

Wrigley Field

> *Replace the scoreboard with a giant slot machine bearing the motto "The City that Works."*

The Museum of Contemporary Art

All exhibited works are to be fastened to the exterior of the building.

The Statue of Goethe

> *Place it atop one of the housing projects at Stateway Gardens, next to a life-sized Mammy-style cookie jar. Have the mayor explain how they are emblems of the city's compassion.*

[40]

Soldier Field

Rename it "Upton Sinclair Field" and convert it into a slaughterhouse. Broadcast images from the stun-line in those television slots formerly devoted to the Bears.

The Art Institute

Leave the artwork on the walls, but convert the interior space into a parking garage for clerical staff working in offices in the Loop.

The Sears Tower

To be used for the anchoring of dirigibles, the only access to the city by air.

Mestrovic's Grant Park Indians

Leave them exactly as they are.

Nightmare, Dream and Bourgeoisie: A Prospect

The War in the Air kept on, until every organized government in the world was as shattered as a heap of china beaten with a stick. The great nations and empires have become but names in the mouths of men. Everywhere there are ruins and unburied dead, and shrunken, yellow-faced survivors in a moral apathy. Here there are robbers, here vigilance committees, and here guerilla bands ruling patches of exhausted territory, strange federations and brotherhoods form and dissolve, and religious fanaticisms begotten in despair gleam in famine-bright eyes.

—H.G. WELLS, HIS NIGHTMARE

The spirit of the new days, of our days, was to be delight in the life of the world; intense and overweening love of the very skin and surface of the earth on which man dwells, such as a lover has in the fair flesh of the woman that he loves; this, I say, was to be the new spirit of the time.

—WILLIAM MORRIS, HIS GREEN DREAM

The spirit of the new days, of our days, would be
here, we dreamed,

with the skin and surface of the earth, in our garden.
Here, where I sit, with the woman that I love.

Here, where delight dwells in the fair flesh of suburban Eden,
where the life of the world is exhausted, and nations

and empires become but names in the mouths of men,
of other men.

The wars reverb in the radio's air around us,
names in the mouths of announcers around the dial. Elsewhere
    there are ruins,

unburied dead, elsewhere guerillas in exhausted territory. And a
voice screeds the fanaticism begotten in gardens much like ours.

Afternoons form
and dissolve, the chipped china of a favorite cup is lifted,

a stick is thrown for a terrier's play, and we ease
to the moral apathy of delight in these our days, delight, in this

our troubled, troubling dream, made up
of where we are, and what we hear.

[43]

Look up each of the quotes

Citation Suite

This is his approach in this poem — may not be necessary

"The poem is not a stream of consciousness, but an area of composition in which I work with whatever comes into it. Only words come into it."

(Robert Duncan)

I. THE SUN, THE CAVE, THE LETTER Z

1.

who? Look up

If thought is like the keyboard of a piano, divided into so many notes, or like the alphabet is arranged in twenty-six letters all in order, then Mr. Ramsay's splendid mind had no sort of difficulty in running over those letters one by one, until it had reached, say, the letter Q. He reached Q. Very few people in the whole of England ever reach Q. But after Q? What comes next? After Q there are a number of letters the last of which is scarcely visible to mortal eyes, but glimmers red in the distance. Z is only reached once by one man in a generation. Still, if he could reach R it would be something. Here at least was Q. He dug his heels in at Q. Q he was sure of. Q he could demonstrate. If Q then is Q...R...

(Virginia Woolf)

Who made your alphabet?

Introduces Q and meaning of Q

The notion of striving for knowledge

2.

Socrates: Imagine the condition of men in a cavernous chamber, underground, with an entrance opening to light, and a length of passage leading in. And here they have been since childhood, chains about their legs and necks, able to face only the darkened wall. A fire burns behind them, and between them and the fire looms a wall, like a screen at the puppet show. And hidden puppet masters make shadow-plays on the dark wall of the darkened cave. Imagine one man, set free of his chains, who turns and walks toward the fire's light, who turns and walks the passage to the scalding sun.

Imagine he called to mind his fellows in their dwelling place, their sad condition.

Glaucon: Yes, I see.

(Plato, in letters I cannot read)

Who dreams beneath your city?

because he's reached letters that are further along the alphabet than the speaker can comprehend?

Introduces story of men who are deprived of the world, and then given the opportunity to reflect'n on it on their world sets up provocative questions in response at the end.

[45]

3.

Mr. Ramsay: Here, we see, is Q.
That we can demonstrate.

Glaucon: Yes, I see.

The sun glimmers red behind the skyline.
The city makes its giant shadow-play.

[handwritten annotation: Adds new information to the quotes]

4.

Imagine Mr. Ramsay in a cavernous chamber,
groping, down a passage, to the light.

Imagine the corridor is longer than he expected.
Imagine him groping there still.

switched Woolfe character into Socrates' story

5.

Or imagine thought a keyboard, or an alphabet.
A man, not Mr. Ramsay, but someone greater

(Plato, say), speaks its letters with a grand enunciation.
A, B, C . . . He sees each, cast in fire, in his mind.
                                    ?

If Q then R. If R then S and T. If T, then, surely, U and V.
(Mr. Ramsay) Yes, I see).   *lifetime reades Z (plato?)*
          — only one man in a lifetime reades Z (plato?)
He reaches Z, here, in our city.
The sun glimmers red behind the skyline.

6.

Who sleeps beneath your city, now?
Homeless, broken, crazy,

down tunnels under Lake Shore Drive,
down in the subways, underpasses—yes, I see.

Yes, there: I can demonstrate.

Who made your alphabet?
There, scrawled on the El train.

Those spray paint letters we cannot read.

Introduces idea that the men in Socrates' story
are homeless,
Also, what if some of the letters of thought
are not found in academic world but
on the streets
contrasts brilliance of thought (in mind)
with other thoughts not captured
by the esoteric (academic?) mind those
of the street (in the flesh)

7.

Imagine, one man reaching Z,
his grand enunciation, his sudden halt—

new letters that he cannot read
stretching, like a keyboard, on and on,

each cast in fire, in its alien shape.
He stands agape, and broken, crazy. He struggles

to mouth their unsaid names. ← *new
Territory*

*The
crazy
man
Thinks*

Blending Plato and the homeless men

[50]

II. NOMAD, GOD AND CITY

1.

—Same? [handwritten annotation: *A bit stilted, mannered*]

London was but a foretaste of this nomadic civilization, which is
altering human nature so profoundly, and throws upon personal
relations a stress greater than any they have ever borne before.
Under cosmopolitanism, if it comes, we shall receive no help
from the earth.

(E.M. Forster) *who?*

Who dreams within this nomad city?   *~ variation from*
Whose city did this Forster dream?   *(p 45) question*
                                      posed after Socrates
                                      quote

A changing social situation

[51]

2.

[handwritten: They set?]

It is with cities as it is with sex. We seek the physical city and find only an agglomeration of private cells. In the city as nowhere else we are reminded that we are individuals, units. Yet the idea of the city remains; it is the god of the city that we pursue, in vain. *[handwritten: weak]*

[handwritten: rush hour?]

Its heart must have lain somewhere. But the god of the city was elusive. The tram was filled with individuals, each man returning to his own cell. *[handwritten: —a bit Leavishanded puv]*

(Naipaul, a nomad come to London) *[handwritten: — is this a real quote?]*

What god do you pursue, in cities?
Who lives within the cell next door? ✓

[handwritten: Thoughts on looking at social forces / ideas and how they disregard the individual & That it is difficult to locate the god (essence) of the city.]

3.

Tired Mr. Ramsay creaks
the tired stairs of his hotel,
he slips the key he's slipped for weeks
in Room Q's lock and leaves the hall.

Some curry cooks on someone's stove
it's someone he will never meet,
he hears a swish—a frayed bathrobe—
the hallway's wandering, bearded Greek.

[handwritten annotations: "Nomad?", "socrates, plato?", "V. Wolf's character again"]

Mr Ramsay pacing restless

4.

Who walks these hallways that wind like a tedious argument?
Who can guess the argument's insidious intent?

Who doubles back in muttering retreats,
eyes odd and elsewhere, pacing where he's paced?

Mr Ramsay — He passes rooms he's passed before,
a letter, painted black, on every door.

thoughts?

[54]

5.

From Socrates quote

In the corridor, insomniac, alone, the Greek dreams of his
    fellows,
their warm dwelling place, and of our nomad city, where he
    lives.

— god of Nomadic city

He imagines the god of cities speaks in notes too deep for
    hearing.
He imagines the god of cities signs a name we cannot read.

He would mouth a prayer.

[55]

6.

What god do you pursue in cities?
Do you see him, briefly, from inside a moving tram?

There—is that his name, those spray paint letters?
Is that him, broken, crazy, speaking tongues?

There, is that him? Can you demonstrate?
Can you mouth or call his unsaid name?

crazy guy

not sure this works

7.

Who dreams, alone, within this nomad city?
Would each wake and know the others
                                            by their names?

[handwritten: homeless ?th]

[handwritten: From p 51]

[handwritten: This section introduces the Greek (Socrates/ Plato?) and the god of the city. They interplay y Mr Ramsey.]

III. THE DREAM OF RUINS —of the West

1.

Imagine that the nations which make up what we call "the West" vanish tomorrow, wiped out by thermonuclear bombs. Only Eastern Asia and sub-Saharan Africa remain inhabitable, and in these regions the reaction to the catastrophe is a ruthless campaign of de-Westernization—a fairly successful campaign to obliterate the memory of the last three hundred years. But imagine also that, in the midst of this de-Westernizing campaign, a few people, mostly in the universities, squirrel away as many souvenirs of the West as they can—as many books, magazines, small artifacts, reproductions of works of art, movie films, videotapes, and so on, as they can conceal. Now imagine that around the year 2500 memory of the catastrophe fades, the sealed-off cellars are uncovered, and artists and scholars begin to tell stories about the West. They will tell many stories . . .

(Richard Rorty, squirreled with all his books, his university)

These stories. *philosopher*

Story of culture wiped out but a trace is kept alive (as an artifact)

mentioned also in
The Colossus ?

2.

→ Two vast and trunkless legs of stone
Stand in the desert . . . Near them, on the sand,
Half sunk, a shattered visage lies, whose frown,   *why rhyme ?*
And wrinkled lip, and sneer of cold command,
Tell that its sculptor well those passions read
Which yet survive, stamped on these lifeless things,
The hand that mocked them, and the heart that fed:
And on the pedestal these words appear . . .

(Percy Shelley, his grand enunciation)

These words.

The ruins of a civilization, the emotion
broken
on a statue's face still show through the
ruins

3.

Mr. Ramsay's visage, shattered, broken, crazy,
his wrinkled lip, his sneer of cold command.

Imagine him in the ruins of our city,
groping down a passage to the light.

Imagine him in the ruins of our alphabet,
his sad condition.

He finds a sealed off-cellar that was buried.
Imagine he makes that cave his hermit's cell.

homeless guy

Mr Ramsay
Touch all previous scenes
Homeless guy

Broken statue
Socrates tale

V. Woolf / Q

Socrates't.lo

*V. Woolf's character now a counterpoint
image to the broken statue
Does Mr Ramsay's face say anything
about his sculptor (god?) ?*

4.

His cave, beneath these trunkless legs of stone,
holds all he's hoarded:

books,
magazines,
small artifacts,
fragments and quotations,
the things he's squirreled away.

He pulls one from the pile to show his young companion.
"Here, we see, is Q"

"Yes," sighs Glaucon, "yes, I see."

Another homeless

Does This mean the Q That is an advanced
Thought?

5.

He builds a small fire in his nomad encampment,
watches shadows play there, on the shattered wall.

The homeless guy is not much
different than the one's chained
to the wall in Socrates' alegory

6.

He would lay his hoarded fragments neatly,
like keys of a piano, side by side,
like letters of lost words he longs to read.

He would mouth these words,
he would mouth a prayer.

idea/image from Woolf now used to
describe homeless men (Keys of piano)

Like a new villanelle

7.

A man, not Mr. Ramsay, dreams a city, its ruined alphabets,
dreams his fellows all as nomads dwelling there.

what does this mean?

Shadows drift across his sleeping visage, → *Is this new?*
→ the grand enunciation of the red and rising sun.

Variation of #1 sec 5

*The death of curiosity +
all moods other than
delight*

IV. The Dream of Fair Flesh and Eden

After the nuclear bombs?

1.

The spirit of the new days, of our days, was to be delight in the
life of the world; intense and overweening <u>love of the very skin</u>
<u>and surface of the earth</u> on which man dwells, such as a lover
has in the fair flesh of the woman he loves; this, I say, was to be
the new spirit of the time. All other moods save this had been
exhausted: the unceasing criticism, the boundless curiosity in
the ways and thoughts of man, which was the mood of the
ancient (Greek,) to whom these things were not so much a means,
as an end, was gone past recovery.

*v. different
from
the
Nomadic
London
that
doesn't
receive
help
From the
earth*

*Third
variation
of
the notion
of
Greek*

(William Morris, his city cold and filled with slow and
drifting shadows; his dream)— *This is W. Morris' dream of
the city*

This, he says:
That we be delivered from our cells and caverns. *of our curiosity*
That we receive help from the earth. *to delight in the world*

This is an opposite view of the dream of ruins

[65]

Reintroduced Alphabet letter
but here they represent names

2.

Sitting, facing the sun, eyes closed
I can hear the sun.
I can hear the birdlife all around for miles . . .
Beyond the birds there are persons
carrying their names like great weights.
Just think, carrying X all your life, or Y or Z . . .
Having to be A all the time or B or C.
Here you can be the sun, the pine, the bird.
You can be breathing.

I tell you, I think this may be Eden,
I think it is.

(Nathaniel Tarn)

poet

What place is gone past all recovery? *– damned?*
What place is lost in all our dreams? *in our dreams of Eden?*

About eliminating names and just being who you are

[66]

3.

If thought is like the keyboard of a piano,
or like an alphabet is arranged in twenty-six letters all in
    order . . .

Mr. Ramsey dreams the keys fly, one by one,
like seagulls disappearing, in the distance and the sun. *Thoughts disappearing*

The Greek's still pacing where he's paced and paced before
when the letters drop from where they hang on every door.
    └ The letters of knowledge

*Note
the
Greek walking
Mr halls (p53)*

*could be about releasing oneself from
the stricture of ordered Thought*

This is the theme of the poem [handwritten annotation]

4.

w Morris [handwritten] *(w. Morris) (Archenbean) p 66* [handwritten] *p 58* [handwritten] *CRooty?* [handwritten]

Imagine that the cities which make up what we call "the West"
vanish tomorrow, gone past recovery, and we are welcomed with
intense and overweening love by the very skin and surface of the
earth, as a lover welcomed to the fair flesh of the woman that he
loves. *(Emfactister) (w. Morris)* [handwritten]

combining 2 quotes [handwritten, left margin]

Paraphrase of p 65 [handwritten, right]

Imagine then our dwelling place—sun, pine, the sound of birds.

I would tell this story.   *p 65*   *N, Totin* [handwritten]

Q [handwritten, circled]

5.

I would catch the words and letters left by others,
lay them, as this story, side by side.

I would dream, here, in my city, in its shadows.
I would be an author with no name.

6.

And if our Mr. Ramsey dropped the weight that is his name?
Would it be him, there, broken, homeless, crazy,

down in the subways, down
the tunnels underneath our Lake Shore Drive?

Would it be him, his author's signature
scrawled on the El train,

those spray paint letters we cannot read?
Would it be him, gone past all recovery? — *Not
sure what this
means*

Would it be him?

*More about identifying and typecasting
some one based on their name. How we use
names to define people yet they are
never the complete description*

[70]

7.

The name of the sleeping man rests on his chest,
it rises and falls with the slowness of his breathing.

The wind moves slowly in low branches, while he dreams.

what dreaming
is he referring to?
p —.'

When you dream you release te
identification with your name

very good

Imitations and Collage: from the Poems of Jules Supervielle

1. PROPHECY
a version of Supervielle's "Prophité"

One day the earth will be a blind space, turning,
Misbreeding night with day.
Under the huge, snow-choked, Andean sky, no mountains.

Of all her houses, a broken terrace;
And of 'the human geography'
Just boundless sorrow.

Of the Atlantic, the merest taste of salt,
And a fish that flies,
Forgetting the vanished sea.

From a carriage of 1905,
Its tall wheels rolling the roadless earth,
Three girls, young, three wraiths of vapor

Will look out, thinking Paris near.
They will find nothing.
Just a cold sky that catches in the throat.

And of all the forests, one bird, singing,
Where none can see or love or hear,
Except a God that, hearing, calls its name.

2. HEART MURMUR
a version of Supervielle's "Coeur"

very nice

A candle is sufficient,
a small fire's light fit for the world

around which your life
shuffles quietly:

a slow, familiar, ambiguous heart,
a serious heart that holds, in your surest self,

a leafless forest,
a horseless highway,

a ship without its crowd of faces,
waves without water.

Then thousands of children pour out
to the square beneath your window

with thin-chested shrieking
till a black-bearded man (where did *he* come from?)

sends them away with a wave of his hand
and, alone again,

your feel your way into your deep flesh,
to a heart nearer its coffin,

a grown man's heart.

3. INSOMNIA
a version of Supervielle's "Insomnie"

These horsemen of a sleepless night
(They can remember nothing)
Brows furrowed, searching—
They cluster, conspire, rally,
Set out to kill your murmurous heart.

How to contain these half-tamed beasts,
Adversaries, chimeras
Set free above the sweat-damp pillow?
Vein-storm blood, quick blood a torrent.
The heart, made dizzy, pretends to stop.

Past-clutched and morning-straining—
Is there a present to this shard of night?
Here we can only deny, renounce,
Here we see ourselves slandered,
Here we are dry wood for fire.

Sleeplessness a sharp stone in our stomachs,
Sleeplessness in our place at the table
Sucking our fears like a chicken bone—
You will probe beneath our skins with knives,
Find what sates you, leave the damp skin's stick and stench.

Let our eyelids close, revealing hollows
That join the body to a hollow depth.
Let the vast night bury us in her indifference,
Let her take us to the sleeper's corridors,
Let the phosphor of our eyes go out.

I don't know those lands and half-made prairies,
The strange and blessed geography
Where dreams and rivers flow without end
Where, at the shores of an ocean, life comes apart
After this blind insomniac wandering.

4. COLLAGE: IN THE KINGDOM OF SELFCONSCIOUSNESS

Here we see ourselves slandered,
Here we are dry wood for fire,

Here the black-bearded king sits high at the table.
He sucks our fears like a chicken-bone. — *repetition*

His gaze catches in our throats,
His gaze a sharp stone in our stomachs.

On the horseless highways, in the leafless forests,
Shuffling with our little candle's flame at night—

Here, where none can see or hear us,
He sees, and hears, and calls our names.

Imitations and Collage: from the Poems
of Blas De Otero

How much are these his poems?

1. FROM EACH ACCORDING TO WHAT HE KNOWS
a version of Otero's "Que Cada Uno Aporte Lo Que Sepa"

It's true, you know: you *can* love a person,
a little toad—don't step on it—

and also a continent like Europe,
always split or wounded or crying horribly.

Some words disturb us, you and me,
"treaty," "theater of operations,"

"end of major fighting," "nothing serious,"
and others too.

But people, they believe all that,
hang bunting, run flags out the windows,

as if it were true,
as if such a thing . . .

It happens—I've seen them myself,
all Easter hats and roses.

In '39 they called the poor men out to Mass,
pulled fuses from a few bombs,

and set off fireworks along the water:
at it again.

After, I heard voices in the next room,
a woman screaming, mad and awful.

We knew,
we knew more than enough.

in grief

2. WORDS GATHERED FOR ANTONIO MACHADO
a version of Otero's "Palabras Reunidas Para Antonio Machado"

> *a solitary heart*
> *is no heart*
>   —A.M.

If I dared
to speak, to call for you . . .
but I am, alone,
no one.

So.
I clench my fists and look to your root-place,
I listen to slow yesterday,
her ballads, all the people's songs—
rough Manrique, exact Frey Luis,
the quick-whip words of old Quevado—
and quick, too,
I touch the earth that has lost you,
and the sea that holds a ship that must find home.

And now,
now the plow has turned in salted soil,
now I'll say *a few true words*,
those with which I first sought a voice:

> *Elm sonorous with wind,*
> *tall poplar, sluggish oak and olive,*
> *trees of a dry land, and of sorrow—*
> *come to clear water, to freedom, to peace*

Sevilla cries. Soria, for once,

grows quiet. Baeza
lifts her sickles to the air, her olive trees
slow-moving to the wind's soft sorrow, which she reaps.
The sea itself falls fast on France to claim you—
it wants,
we want,
to have you here,
        to share you out
like bread.

3. THE CLOISTER OF SHADOWS
a version of Otero's "El Claustro de las Sombras"

> *... to the antique order of the dead*
> FRANCIS THOMPSON

Just now I have thirty-three years piled on my study table
and a few months left over in the silver ashtray.
I've put this question to my sisters: do you know this man
between my left and right shoulders? He goes where I go,
and turns his face if I turn mine ...

I grow cold, and don't know what to wear
beneath this cloaking death, don't know what plot of earth is mine,
what night I should prepare,
what green and silent ocean waits ...

Sometimes I'd be a brother of the ancient order of the dead
and serve in silence; meditate in a corner of the dead,

in the cloister of shadows, there,
where dreams rise guileless in the smoky light.

nice wrap up

4. Collage: The Public Life

If you reap a soft, slow moving sorrow,
If you gather years in a silver ashtray,

If you wait, a green and silent ocean, *# 3*
If you serve the antique order of yourself,

If, at your study table,
you know, you know too much—

can you love a person, or a continent? *# 1*
Can you turn and share yourself like bread?

The Frozen Thames

a Stuart broadsheet poem, here reworked

1.

Great Britain's Wonder, London's Admiration
Being The True, The Exact Representation

Of the late, unparrallell'd, Prodigious Frost

which, begun about the beginning of *December* 1693,
continued till the Fourth Day of *February* following, And held
on with such violence, that Men and Beasts, Coaches and
Carts, went as frequently thereon, as Boats were wont to pass
before.

From Southwark to the Temple, from one year's shortened days
Into the next, from the printer's press and pages,
For half a penny in the market stall
For the wall above the hearth-space,
For a season's admiration,
For curiosity, for keepsake, by curator, donor, don and queue,
By dealer and restorer's smoothing hand,
By chance,

This print, *The Frozen Thames*, displayed.

There you may see the coaches swiftly run
As if beneath the ice were waters none.

And there, below the pictured river,
read:

Behold the Wonder of this present Age,
A Famous RIVER now become a Stage.

[84]

2.

A stage,
on which the players play:

There,
> Bulls they bait

There
drink to excess

> Man (out-tippling of the fishes) reels

There
— Ice Skates →

> Dutchmen in their nimble cutting Scates
> To please the crowd, do show their Tricks and Feats

There

> You may see small vessels under sail
> All's one to them, with or against the gale
> And as they pass they little guns do fire
> Thereby alerting all they are for hire.

These are Archambeau's rhymes

Reel and skate here in this Thames:

> Here is also a lottery and Music new
> The Thames is now both *Fair* and *Market* too.
> There is such Whimsies on the Frozen Ice
> Makes some believe the Thames a Paradice.

Coals being dear are carry'd on men's backs

3.

Man reels. To please the crowd
Do show their tricks and feats. As they pass
Their little guns they fire.
Or did,
or rather did.

For play the guns they fire, for play
And cash, for play a music new, a lottery
For half a penny many more, for play
And cash, they make both *Fair* and *Market* too.
Or did, or rather did.

The play long stopped, new music old, a fortune won
And then forgot, ice melted into water dark below.

And yet

(a wonder, and an admiration)
the Dutchmen play, here, skate and laugh.

4.

To say, somewhat banally, art survives.
To say, somewhat banally, rivers freeze.

The river froze. The art survives
(The Dutchmen on their nimble skates)
(By curator, donor, don,
              by chance)

As if beneath the ice were waters none.
As if beneath the clear sheet of museum glass
The sheet of paper
The lines on which we skate
Were waters none

No cold, no movement, darting life
That's gone.

To say, somewhat banally, that we die.
That what is frozen in a sheet will pass away.

[handwritten annotations:]

Lines from previous sections repeated. Give the effect of summarizing and it creates some force. and mystery. As though all these disparate presentations are linked by an idea

[left margin annotation:] written lines

[right of "To say... that we die" line, with arrow:] Nice build on the repetition to "up the ante" with a deeper idea

[87]

5.

To say: this sheet's
A record, skater's lines cut into ice,

To say: Tricks and Feats are what survive.
To say:

And all the world a frozen Thames,
And you, a Dutchman skating there. ← The implication:
we are all
skating on thin ice

This happened at the carnival on the ice?

6.

Read:

    Here roasted was an *Oxe* before the Court

Read:

    This is the Booth, where *Tea* and *Rum* abounds

Read:

    This is the *Printing-Booth*, of wondrous Fame
    Because each Man in there did print his *Name*

For play. For cash.
And each did print his name.

For what survives.

7.

To make of frost a holiday (and money,
Money too), they built their booths upon the ice.

When coaches ran where boats did go.
When printer's cold hands worked the press.

When guns were shot (for cash, for play)—
They laughed and skated on that ice.

And here, on this, our frozen Thames,
Our city—fair and market, too—

With tea and rum and wondrous crowds,
Here, may we skate upon this ice,

May we believe (what tricks, what feats)
This Thames, our Thames, our paradise.

A lyric but a bit of a small ending

Major Thel:
A Space Oddity

In the key of Bowie, to the tune of Blake.

THEL'S MOTTO

Four . . .
Does Houston know what re-entry is like?

Three . . .
Or will you ask John Glenn?

Two . . .
Can Wisdom be stored in a network hub?

One . . .
Or Love in a meg of ram?

FOUR . . .

Ground Control to Major Thel . . .
This is Ground Control to Major Thel . . .   Bowie! Thin, white dude

Young, seraphic, androgyne, the thin white astronaut, our Thel.
Adona I's the mission. Earthward the capsule falls.

Ground Control to Major Thel . . .
This is Ground Control to Major Thel . . .

paraphrase of poem

"Why fade the planet's lotus-blossom children, born but to
   smile, dance and fall?"
Thel's raving, sir. Just let it go. O_2's been low a while.

Thel's reflection in the porthole swirls.
Fireflies zigzag, stardust twirls. Thel's visage is a boy's—no: thin
   vision of a girl.   rhymes

A smallish reddish meteor, racing past the porthole, answers our
   intrepid Major:

The meteor speaks

"A rock-chunk, scudding earthward, I;
   but it's all good.

They told me, hey, you'll hit the outer atmosphere and
      skip a while,
   light up, burn bright,

splashdown in the blue orb's ocean, scrapped. What's left?
Dust drifting in the sweet eternal waves. Lapped on the
      shores where

music plays. Eternal in a grain of sand, that's me.
And, worse-case wise, you too, my Major, my sweet Thel."

Thel, trembling, wan and pallid, speaks: *a reversal from what she's called in the poem*

"Oh little virgin of the peaceful skies,
giving yourself as auger's-light, telescope-delight,

and beach-sand for the sweet-sunned rasta-times—
for you, it's all good, I concede. But Thel?

I crash this can and vanish.
Who'll find my corpse beneath the waves?"

"Talk to the clouds," said the meteor, streaking down
in the general direction of Fire Island, "they'll set you straight."

Thel's dream-eyes turn to planet earth, whose cloud-curves coalesce.
A moon-man face of vapors winks, broad-smiling, breathes and says . .
            .

Ground Control to Major Thel . . .
This is Ground Control to Major Thel . . .

THREE . . .

Thel shakes it off. No cloud's called Ground Control. Not one.
"Oh little globe of clouds, come tell young Thel up in this can,

why you don't cry. You fade.
Your vigor is vapor, gone as soon as made.

Gone as I am, when I steer this broken capsule back to earth.
Splashed-down and drowning, fit fodder for a tombstone epitaph—

What gives?"

    The clouds, mass-morphing, still reply:
    "Oh, you know. I condense and rain.

    Or I sneak down and court the soft-skinned dew,
    the doe-eyed virgin on her trembling knees.

    We rise together in the morning in a golden band
    and never part. Unless her father's around.

    We walk united, bearing food to all the tender flowers.
    You should try it sometime. I've got her number."

Thel's androgyne pale brow is knit with fret.
The cloud speaks straight and true and well, and yet . . .

"I feel that I am not like thee—I feed no little flowers from up here . . ."
Thel glances at the gauge marked, simply, "air."

Two . . .

The needle of the air gauge quivers, until Thel
sees it as a cartoon worm (air-loss: our brave astronaut's not well).

The worm's voice is an infant's, lisping and, arguably, insipid:

> "Oh beauty of all pale-young androgynes,
> we live not for ourselves. No way. There's
>
> the whole cycle-of-life thing. And it's not so bad,
> really. So come back home and join the party. Gender,
>
> generation, feast and be fed on. It's time to leave
> that capsule if you dare. If not, you're going to end up—
>   where?

Ground Control to Major Thel . . .
This is Ground Control to Major Thel . . .

ONE . . .   *stilted diction, why?*

Thel gets it straight, both eyes <u>unclosed to their destruction</u>. The   *interesting*
earth below, its knots of vegetation, roots wound through   *concept*
skeletons, blossoms feeding hummingbirds. Books read in
college, then forgot, then <u>fizzing</u> back to life <u>in how one speaks</u>
<u>or lives or wants to live or</u> write. Styles that die and come again,
made different from themselves, modified in the guts of the
living. The music left unplayed for years now heard in someone
else's singing. Perhaps one thing's midwife to the other, when it
comes. All one, the flux of clouds. *This*, weirdly new and old and
blooming, flowers out from *that's* soft dying-bed.

But not for Thel, no not for Thel, no not for virgin Thel.

This is Ground Control to Major Thel . . .

[96]

IN ELSINORE

THIS MONUMENT ERECTED IN LOVING MEMORY OF

THE ACADEMIC LEFT OF THE NINETIES,

MY PEOPLE

WHO DID GOOD WORK BUT DESERVE A KICK OR TWO FOR
GROWING PIOUS IN THEIR LITTLE CORNERS OF POWER AND
PRIVILEGE DON'T YOU AGREE REALLY DON'T YOU FROM TIME
TO TIME?

1. Osric, Medievalist, Junkets to Kalamazoo

[handwritten: why the ancients fiction?]

Come see the good Prof. Rosencrantz. Come, *do* *[handwritten: sword]*
meet gentle Guildenstern. Rapier-wearing medievalists
arrived in this mad north (north midwest):
they'd fear a goose-quill, lest it pen a snide review.
A Lenten entertainment, this, I know—
minds grown too narrow for their small ambitions, *[handwritten: Bitter accusatory]*
Innovations trumped by inhibitions—
all Denmark's just a prison: read Foucault. *[handwritten: ?]*
But prison beats my fate: I'll be on ice *[handwritten: steward]*
if they turn down "Chaucer's Gendered Manciple" *[handwritten: too pitying]*
for their lick-ass trendy P.C.-pissing journal
Premodern Discursivity. Play nice.
God save you sirs! My honored lords! What's new?
How happy first to think on, then see, *you*!

2. Profs. Rosencrantz and Guildenstern: The Promotions and Tenure Committee

Total Kiss-ass

Here on this boat to England (the land where dwells the Dean)—
on this boat, and not to rock it, we.
Sooth! Footfalls on the deck! The Chair is seen!
God save you, noble sir, your voice-mail and your e.
How speak *we* of our Hamlet, young and brave?
How speak you first? Or no? Oh come do say!
Opine your August self before speak we.
He's . . . great and noble? No? He's but a knave?
His research, sir, is great, if by great mean we small,
or smaller still, or not at all. But on all the great committees he has sat,
and sat he has, until the meeting's done, then wandered down the hall.
But teaching! There's the thing. His teaching heals all other ills,
for being good, if by good we mean . . .
We'll bear your solemn letter to the Dean.

3. Hamlet, Denied Tenure

Oh howl in the graveyard. Fuck.
Alas, Prof. Hamlet (assistant prof)
you hardly knew what smacked you,
snapped the golden cord of tenure-track
ascent. I'll talk to myself, 'cause the world
ain't listening. My gorge rims at the thought
of these six years. "The chairman comes!
Oh, genuflect, before his tweed, his tenure
and his tricks!" "Good morrow, dearest colleague,
how dost the book? How went the class?"
My skull's tongue once could sing
or kiss an ass. For what? They sing
at making graves, when making mine.
It's shuffle off to Idaho, to grunt
and sweat a one-year gig, a state
from which no traveler returns.
They pour their poison in my ear,
their careful letter's all-too-clear:
My job, my place, my fated spot
dispelled, to fund a theory slot.

[100]

4. OPHELIA MAKES DEAN

Dean or Queen, that's my scene.
My act, my scene, my line. Act!
Not like that limp-dick prettyboy,
who thought I'd pine for love. Now
love, sweet love, hey there's a line,   *he can't help himself*
they'd feed you that, a line, a load,   *rhyme, alleteration*
a loathsome toad. Drowned in tears
and river-reeds, not me! That
pre-feminist reading leaves me cold
as clay, and buried there. Now watch
as Hound-dog Hammie chaws his bones
and howls in the graveyard. Putz.
Act! From the margins of the text
to the corridors of power, ivy-clad   *King in Hamlet*
and mine mine mine. Smooth Fortinbras,
(oh bray and bellow, Fortinbras,
oh preen and puff) struts pretty
by the stagelights, rolls off me in the sack.
He's mine, my model, mode, my sworded mate.   *rhyme*
I'm his new Queen, made Dean of late.

[Hamlet character: key advisor to King Claudius
egotistical, simple?]

5. POLONIUS EMERITUS

Oh, she's scant enough of maiden presence
now, that girl, scant of maidenhood and—head.
Vulgar, she, and not familiar. You'd think
she'd call. Off with that swagger-Swede, endowed
chair Euro-trash, I'm sure I'm sure. And me?
A sigh, a cup of tea, a putter through the bookshelves,
so. Don't think the arras of seniority's worth much.
Neither an adjunct nor a graybeard be:
they'll steamroll both. Stalwart
to a dead king gets you squat.
Think they'd ask me what I think?
Oh not quite so. At tenure-time young Hamlet
gets the chuck. My sage opinion?
Truth-trust of kings, close counsel
of the Queen's last consort too, and no one asked . . .
A sigh, a cup of tea, a putter through the bookshelves,
so. To Italy next summer? A think-tank talk?
A book? My publisher wants racy stuff, not mine.
The new-hatch'd, unfledged colleagues pass me by,
stalk by my corner office vulture-eyed.

The Poet, as Professor, Dreams

in penance for ironic Elsinore, this sentiment...

In his dream the professor sees his words as they billow out
and over his hunched students, to cluster high in the rafters of
   the lecture hall.

He sees as phrases rise from all the college buildings, up from the
chimneys to the cold and hardened sky. The wind catches them,
all those thin and fraying vapors, and takes them, tears them,
bears them south, toward the city.

They will scatter like scraps of litter among tall buildings.

Perhaps one will catch on a window pane, distract the room's one
dweller, for a while, before gusting out to the wind-ruffed lake.

Perhaps some will cluster like fall leaves in the gutters.

Perhaps someone will bend to pick one up.
Perhaps it is the professor stooping, grown old.
Perhaps it is a student, young or growing old.
Perhaps someone will bend to pick one up, in a mittened hand,
put it in a pocket, keep it there.

Perhaps, dreams the professor, that word will be his.

if There more 2 of me and one of you
it would be very jealous

Printed in the United States
24184LVS00002B/34-42

9 781844 710492